Awake: A Dream

Elise Timm-Bottos

BookLeaf
Publishing

Presentation by *BookLeaf Publishing*

Web: www.bookleafpub.com

E-mail: info@bookleafpub.com

ISBN: 978-93-95890-28-1

First edition 2022

*To my dog, Ella Indigo Oakley, who loves me
on my worst days.*

ACKNOWLEDGEMENT

Thank you to my dear mom who helped me edit, you are truly the best mom I could ask for.

Thanks to everyone who helped me through this difficult journey; Everyone on the Bus Crew; you know who you are, my roomies for watching my dog, the kitchen crew for feeding me, the RV crew who saved us, and for everyone else who helped us while we were sick or struggling, thank you thank you thank you.

PREFACE

I did not know what this book would be when I signed up for this writing challenge, but the premise seemed simple enough. Write a poem a day for the length of the challenge. I knew I was going to Burning Man and I figured it would make for an interesting story. I did not know what I was about to go through and how challenging this adventure would be for me. Here it is, in all its messy glory, my journey to Black Rock City.

Dream of a Dust Storm and the Breeze -Aug 16 2022

Packing for Burning Man is like
playing darts in a dark room.
Will I have a sunburn, rash, eye sore, toe bleed?
How can one prepare for it all?
Any and all ailments in an unforgiving desert.
Fun is easier
bubbles, fans, multiple silly hats
a new hat for each day.
It is like life
Every day a mix of grinding and pushing
working your fingers to the bone
and then, enough, stop. relax.
Walking out into the sun
and feeling it on your skin.

Up and Att'em -Aug 17 2022

Why am I so sad?
Is it my recent breakup?
The death of my father, and my grandmother?
The impending doom of climate change
and no clear path to a career I love?
Maybe I am just hungry
or need a little more sleep.
Sleep for ten more hours, 100 days,
ten years and still wake up tired
and sad
ready to greet the day.

Miraculous Things -Aug 18
2022

There are stories about people
who do miraculous things.
Climb mountains, find treasures,
swing from trees.
Are there times those people
feel as small as me?
One floating particle on an endless sea?

There are stories about people
who go through incredible hardship.
Climb out the other side,
ready to burn more brightly, give out more
find their fire in the world.
How to trust that that will be me?
To come back fiercer, then when I left.

That Dream -Aug 19 2022

I had that dream again -with you-
sitting in your basement, talking.
We were broken up
but your mom invites people over
to meet me and introduces me as
your girlfriend.
Oh, you didn't tell her, I realize,
now it's too late and too awkward.
We shrug and laugh a little
unsure of who we are now
to each other.

I Love My House -Aug 20 2022

Today is finally the big day,
gathering up and starting to move
to Portland, to Mt. Shasta, to Black Rock City.
My gut cramps.
Here's to unknown waters
Big Things.
Doing what scares us.
Here's to jumping in, when staying at home
would be easier.
I will miss my dog and my bed,
and my cream of Earl Grey tea every morning.
Has Covid made us all creatures of comfort?
I will miss my window view,
how the sun spills over the pine-filled
mountains,
but will I miss my old self more?

Enough Healing Salve for All
-Aug 21, 2022

Last night, after a long windy car drive,
we arrived at Mythmaker's camp.
The preparation of a Viking mead hall,
giant puppets and supplies,
were spilling out of a double decker stage,
on a school bus, all undeniably cool.
We are trying to frantically finish
roll up our tents up and find a spot on the bus
and we only have until 5 to finish,
not that anyone is counting.

The feeling the gratefulness consumes me,
to be out and exploring,
to be alive, to find comradery after feeling so
isolated
to have some time,
to let old wounds heal.
It is like a thick healing salve,
or resting after running,
or letting a breath out
you didn't know you were holding in.

This Viking Bus -Aug 22-23, 2022

The bus, repainted black and green,
With accents of two gold dragons
(I had the honour of painting yesterday),
Inside, a community home,
Lush red velvet cushions, wooden dressers,
A menagerie of Burning Man What When
Where
Books, Viking Lore, Medallions, Word Magnets
stuck to the ceiling.
It is a dreamy, colourful, comfy place.
My hands are filthy from lifting and packing
fire props and fire dragons for our show.
Black metal, dusty and sharp.

We worked all day in a baking sun,
loading up the stage, the bikes, the luggage
This massive dragon beast of a bus,
draws attention everywhere she goes.
we drove wildly through Oregon, stopping in
Medford,
to meet some new people who felt like old
friends.
They were so sweet,

giving us batteries, pins, beautiful rocks and
more
Their enthusiasm was pulpable and it was
catching.

Hush Hush -Aug 24, 2022

Yesterday tested everyone's limits but
today we spun mercilessly out of control
a whispered word? a look.
Suddenly we are no longer a merry crew
united under one fearless leader.

Harsh words needlessly spread
yet we are all still here, too late to
back out now.
What are you bringing to the table?
Is it years of your own unworth?
Is it two hours of unprocessed trauma,
that you need us all to listen to?
Our trust was building but then
you broke it.

Today I am sad and tired.
The merry glow of a grand adventure
has completely faded.
Instead I am left dreaming.
I was somewhere else
Somewhere less uncontrollable
Somewhere safer, like my home.

We are not at Mt. Shasta yet
I am not ready for ritual.
I am not ready for another day
of this unrelenting bullshit.
Have you ever pleased a
certified narcissist?
Yea, me neither.

Breaking Open Old Wounds
-Aug 24, 2022

You screamed at my friend
for taking too long trying to buy a camping mat
from Walmart,
and this is after you told her,
not to worry about time,
that everyone was moving slowly.
That is a contradiction.
You then made us listen to you vent
for two hours in the parking lot,
wasting everyone's time.
That was also a contradiction.
You told us if we are waiting for you,
it's good.
but if you are waiting for us,
it's bad.
It is really bad.
Anxiously waiting, for someone to speak up,
before you blow up again
on someone else undeserving of your fury.
And on this bus full of amazing, loving,
hardworking people
I have never felt more alone or unsafe.

We are in this liminal moment,
a bus unlike any other,
whirling down the highway
and our anger and drama
is quickly wisped to the wind,
thrown out on the highway,
never to be seen again.
That is, unless we keep it with us
which is my choice.
I erase the frustration of yesterday
and I find peace within myself.

Many Days, No Water -Aug 25-26, 2022

Wow! One day had passed but feels like years,
we stopped to camp instead of driving
recklessly through the night.
My whole body is sore.
Haven't showered in four days,
things are getting ripe.
Yesterday at Mt. Shasta I ran
into the water with all my clothes on,
and within minutes, my long red skirt
was dry.
Lets get some Europeans from the Walmart
parking lot,
where they have been stranded for a day,
and get the fuck to playa.

First Thoughts Arriving to Playa:

Wow, this is fucking crazy
Wow, WE are fucking crazy.
How can the people I am travelling with never
sleep?
They are starting the build as we arrive.
Maybe I am a sparkle pony

because I physically and mentally can do no
more.
So I set up camp on the side to rest
and tomorrow I will bake in the sun.
Just kidding! Man with microphone blasting my
tent. I am awake, and help until it is done.

Somewhere Other than Earth
-Aug 27, 2022

Things are otherworldly here
the normal has left without a goodbye
who looks like a hero?
who looks like a devil?
Are we meeting a reflection of ourselves?

Cool things I've seen:
two light up giraffes
a penis in spaghetti painting
the start of a Viking Village

Update: Burning up, my stomach is fucked and I
am dying, let this be my last Will and Testament:

To my dad on the day of my death:
Watching you slip away
was like watching the moon fade.
Unforgettable and transient.
I am awed by your magnificent presence
that was here and then gone.
How enormous and precious every
moment we love.
I am trying to find the words
to say how much I miss you

and miss the simplicity of my life
before you died.
Because, really, afterwards everything
got so much worse
and I am still reeling, reeling,
hoping, somehow, to find my footing again.

Waking Nightmare -Aug 28, 2022

I am slowly recovering
from the worst stomach pains
vomiting and diarrhea I've ever had
The med tent (best free health care in America.
ha.)
thinks it was a stomach bug and pumps with
water.
So far, I've seen the med tent and my tent
and today is the first day of Burning Man:
Waking Dreams
Burning Man 2022: Waking Nightmare

I don't think I have ever felt less prepared
I am so weak and have a huge headache
I'm not even sure if I have much else to say
besides fuck my burn.

I Have Burned the Poem -Aug 29, 2022

I have burned the poem I wrote today,
(it was put in an envelope
to be burned in the temple.)
which you were probably hoping to read.

I guess no one will ever read it,
instead you just get this note

so simple
so quick

Plague Update (I am MOOP) -Aug 30, 2022

The plague of the stomach virus
has infiltrated our camp
and now 14 people have ended up in the med
tent.
At least they are prepared for them.
I guess I am still waiting for some magic to
happen,
Yes, I've met some nice people and seen some
cool things,
but the insanity of this place is still too much.

Why the fuck am I even here?

Feeling Better -Aug 31, 2022

Trying on a bustle for my pirate costume
when I heard someone say "Balkan Bump"
one of my new favourite artists
I found out they were playing at Ego Trip,
wandered over and asked the bartender if Balkan
Bump was playing
and he said "yes, and he's sitting right here"
We talked a little bit and then he said, "oh, guess
I should go play"
and he went on to play the most amazing set
and I danced my heart out and felt so free.

There's some magic here after all

Then I rode on a giant fish art car to a fire show
to eat poutine.
Can't make this stuff up.

Today is my Birthday- Sept 1 2022

I feel alone.
My morning started with another angry meeting
from our nightmare leader.
not even a happy birthday before the guilt trip.
and yet, I keep finding what I am looking for.
a hug, a cuddle.
A nice deep talk!
A pink bicycle parade where we tell everyone "I
love you" as we ride by
 hugging so many strangers!
Awwwwwww
Today is my birthday and I watched
Thunderdome fights,
I felt fear and madness passing through me like
fire,
all this fury at being fully alive.

Burning Man -Sept 2, 2022

If I could, I would switch today to be my real
birthday,
only one day difference,
yet I am pretty sure this is how Burning Man is
supposed to be.
We went to Scar Bar, a drink for every story of a
scar you have.
We drew farm animals on a big structure, ate
cheeseburgers and confusing chips,
We went to FOMO camp and got cured of our
FOMO
and I adopted a mutant monkey and was finally
happy.
I felt a group surrounded me, protected me from
all the uncertainty.
Like how will we get away from that nasty man?
How are we going to make it home?

Finding Happy -Sept 3, 2022

Last night was truly incredible.
Happy and I explored everywhere on our bikes
finding new places even a block from our camp.
We acted like old lovers who had known each
other forever.
We had spicy pickle shots,
got shibari rope tops,
explored our sexuality,
danced everywhere,
watched the sun come up on a magic carpet.
It was nice to feel loved if even for one night,
you know?
to feel trusted and good.
I have been too reliant on a partner to feel safe,
a trait I picked up from my mother.
I am sorry, mom, I have to be more reliant on
myself.
Tonight, we watch our friends in a fire show,
and then the man burns.

A Kind of Serenity -Sept 4, 2022

I went to the temple
and felt so overwhelmed.
So many messages and gifts to people who have
died,
written and drawn all over the walls.
It was a sacred space built out in the middle of
nowhere.
Too bad with all our uncertainty we couldn't
stay to watch it burn.
But I felt it, burning away, thawing my grieving
heart.

We lose Happy early in the night
and still ride around, giggling and giddy
rocking our freedom.
The lights and trippy art cars are
supremely confusing at night
we get lost and find each other again.
I have so much to be thankful for and the desert
has humbled me.

Losing Happy -Sept 5, 2022

I cannot wait to get home.
We drove and drove and waited 8 hours in
Exodus.
Everyone in this crew is exhausted and trying to
keep it together.
Happy and I are back to being complete
strangers
Did we really share some magical nights
together?
I am disheartened, when we get where we are
going, we probably wont see each other again.
I practise the buddhist/bullshit art of letting go.

Familiar Things- Sept 6, 2022

We have arrived back to Portland
and the insanity of Burning Man begins to fade.
This project we can do,
we clean our stuff,
unload the cube van,
get our things and return home.
Step by step the world returns to familiar and I
am glad.
I am tired, disappointed and sad.

Reflect, Respect, Repent, Regret -Sept 7, 2022

Walk around me lover sunshine,
your rays are hardly mine.
I walk the streets in starry gaze
its easier to be amazed
as the glowsticks start to fade
we are left with the remains.
To hope, to cope, to find our dope,
our tropes to let us know our own.
I am amazed you actually stayed
and filled up your own cup.
My cup is empty, as I said,
too embarrassed to turn red, and yet
I bet you know
that cup is beautiful.
So please, squeeze tight,
with all your might
and show me what is Love
Is it hidden far away?
Is it ever here to stay?
Will it show me what I want?
Will it take from me what it ought?
Reflect, Respect, Repent, Return
Relearn, Unfurl, Uncurse your Burn.

Tick Tock -Sept 10, 2022

As Time turns back to
a steady Tick Tock Tick Tock
and all my worries unfurl like
a red carpet at my feet
I begin to see the little joys
I have so often taken for granted.
Nothing like almost dying of dehydration
in the Nevada desert to make you
wake up and smell the beautiful roses.
Nothing like it, they say,
Burning Man,
Go there to have your soul turned inside out and
dusted
Go there for grand dreams and nightmares,
because bad dreams are still dreams,
something shifting in your unconscious.
Am I a burner after all this, no, no, I don't think
so.
I am human, I am heart, I am a soul on Earth.